I CAN DO IT!
I CAN DO IT!
Arts & Crafts for the Mentally Retarded. By
SUE WILSON

The Quail Street Publishing Company
Newport Beach, California

Library of Congress Catalog Card 76-14563

ISBN 0-89307-002-5

Introduction

This is a book of experiences—easy, difficult, long, short, imperfect, joyous. They've been compiled over several years of art and craft work with our retarded daughter, Leslie, and with many other handicapped children and adults.   They've been tested at home and also in schools, but are offered as ideas and not hard-and-fast rules. Every time one of these projects was repeated, it was different—just as the children were different or had new feelings about it.

The most successful projects have been selected, success being measured by the satisfaction children expressed over them. Sometimes the finished products were important; more often, the greatest pleasures seemed to come in the making process. Right-handed, left-handed, with good vision, with poor vision, with perceptual problems, with all sizes and shapes of brushes and drawing tools, with special scissors and enormous amounts of patience (on everybody's part), retarded children continued to bring forth surprises. We had a good time, too!

Most children follow a prescribed route in art work, starting with playful scribbling around the age of two. This usually develops into object painting, then into an attempt to communicate what they see to others. Feelings and fantasy begin to appear, and with increased socialization, many enjoy group projects. Craftwork becomes important and some enjoy "junk art"—assembling scrap objects into designs and patterns, in both two and three dimensions. In the teens, using specific techniques (like sculpting and silk-screening) can bring satisfaction and a sense of accomplishment in finished work. These general phases stop and start and overlap, pointing to stages of mind and muscle development. An enjoyment of design spans all of them.

Retarded children, especially those with brain damage, may follow zig-zag routes—which is what makes their art and craft work so exciting! An older child who has never done art work may scribble in paint one day and start painting faces a few days later! Some may not be able to tackle subject matter of any kind, but they'll produce beautiful flowing designs in unique styles. The surprises go on and on.

Start wherever a child is. If he or she is provided with things like large papers, varieties of paints and working materials, clay and gluing opportunities, it won't matter whether they can only make circles with eye dots or lines which loop around and around in a repeated pattern. Gradually, you'll begin to see an emerging style and a sense of pleasure in the artwork itself. (You may see an improvement in schoolwork or general coordination, too.) Some retarded children are natural painters, illustrators, cartoonists, printmakers, sculptors and weavers, but they'll never discover it unless they've been exposed to the materials and the experience!

The most difficult areas of work can be those which involve concepts and planning. In spite of this, we've made kites and linoleum block prints and batiks, moving slowly step-by-step, sometimes taking days (ten minutes one day, 15 the next and so on depending upon the individual child).

Generally, our experience has been that a half-hour of art or craft work may be long enough, especially at the beginning. (It tends to build, like exercising.) If 15 minutes is enough, stop at that. If someone wants to go longer, that's all right, too, as long as there are rest or exercise breaks for those who need them. Safety is the first prerequisite; working success is the second. At the first sign of hazard, struggle or unwillingness, we stopped what we were doing, changed it, adapted it or just put it aside for a while.

Let a retarded child do as much of his or her own work as possible, but be ready to pre-cut, pre-glue, pre-sew or pre-whatever's necessary. Don't let the difficult appearance of a project hold you back, either—or an illustration that looks too finished. We've found that painting can be enjoyed by anyone who can move a brush across paper, and the same thing is true of craft work. There may be enormous benefit in letting someone do just part of a project and while subject matter is shown as a guide, it isn't needed. Pleasure in using materials may be far more important. In the beginning, some children may have trouble just holding a brush or dipping it into paint. Lead gently. Experience will build upon experience and skills will follow.

Whatever a child's mental age or skill level, scrap supplies are important to keep on hand. Build a collection from your own household, or several households. Commercial firms may have cast-offs to add, too. What are some of these things? Beads, buttons, string, ribbon, yarn, cloth scraps, gift wrapping papers, styrofoam packing material, corks, interesting sticks and pebbles, seed pods, cardboard cylinders, small boxes, bits and ends of broken toys, nuts, bolts, berry boxes and so on. Ways to use these materials are almost endless, from collaging to clothes decoration!

Keep magazine cut-outs on hand, too—as many as possible. All kinds will do, especially those from glossy colored pages. Store them in folders or filing boxes or in any way that's convenient, as long as they're quickly available for reference. It's helpful to catagorize them as you cut them out, grouping pictures under "People," "Flowers," "Birds," "Ocean Scenes,""Food" and whatever else you want.

Advertising brochures and store mailers are useful, too, and all kinds of things showing pattern can be tucked in a "Designs" folder. This kind of file can be a valued resource for one individual or several. Some children will use the pictures for reference or ideas in painting. Others can glue them directly on paper, wood or some other working surface. The more pictures you can collect, the better.

There are numerous follow-up books on art and art techniques in the library. For someone who wants to look more into craft work, there are also excellent books and probably local instructors who can give first-hand help. Woodwork, metalwork, leatherwork, ceramics, stained glass, jewelry making (with tools like jewelers' saws), toymaking, loomwork and plastics are only a few of the crafts available in most areas. Retarded children and adults have done all of them and done them beautifully.

For simplification, the following text is addressed directly to the reader—parent, teacher, friend or retarded child who is able to read and follow instructions. Although the pages are coded, help and concern for safety are implied all the way through. So are sincere encouragement and praise—lots of it! More than anything else, retarded children need to feel accepted and enjoyed. They want their work to be accepted and enjoyed, too.

Ultimately, as Norman LaLiberte says, nothing is a mistake. There's no win and there's no fail. There's only the making, the act of creating—and therein lies the joy.

Wherever you are, you're wished great pleasure in the experiences ahead!

Table of Contents

Project Descriptions

Time estimates are (S) - short, 15 minutes or less; (V) - variable, depending upon the individual, roughly a half-hour; (L) - long, one hour or more of working time.

To LESLIE
and many, many
others

7

The ideas and projects in this book are coded. These symbols are repeated on each page for easy reference. TMR stands for trainable mentally retarded, EMR for educable mentally retarded.

The first two symbols are meant only as a general guide. A severely handicapped child may be able to breeze through one of the advanced projects—another with good coordination may have trouble with fingerpaint! Take individual differences and attention spans into account. In this field of surprising accomplishments, there are very few, if any, rules.

 For anyone, including TMR

 Extra effort, usually (but not always) for EMR

 Uses mostly small muscles.

 Uses large muscles.

 May need lots of help (with materials or project or both)

 Step-by-step, hawk eye supervision

 Caution—see note on the same page

TIME ESTIMATES

 S short project, 15 minutes or less

V Variable, depending upon the individual—plan on half an hour as a starter

L Long, one hour or more

These are actual working times. A project may be spread over two or three days, allowing paint to dry, etc.

9

TEMPERA

POWDERED TEMPERA

ACRYLIC PAINT

ACRYLIC PAINT

PURE PIGMENT

Different Kinds of paint and how to use it

TEMPERA Most of the ideas on the next few pages call for tempera. Almost everybody likes this paint. It's thick and bright and flows easily across the paper to make exciting pictures. It has a water base and washes easily off hands and out of hair and even off clothes (but don't let it dry too long!).

Tempera comes ready mixed and in powder form to be mixed with water until thick and creamy. The pre-mixed paint is brighter and usually gives better results. It's first choice. (Use powdered tempera for things like finger paint and when you have large areas to cover.) Buy either kind in an art supply store.

This paint may rub off or fade after a long period of time. Protect it with a coating of varnish, spray varnish, liquid floor wax or even colorless nail polish—depending on what it's covering.

Use tempera for beginning art projects. It comes in lots of colors. The basic five are red, yellow, blue, black and white. You can mix <u>almost</u> any other colors from these five. If possible, add green, turquoise and magenta to your shopping list. In this kind of paint, the commercial green has a freshness that's hard to mix. The same thing is true of turquoise, especially for sunny blue skies and oceans. Commercial magenta is **special**, too. Mix some white into it and watch for a brilliant lush strawberry-ice-cream pink! (It's hard to mix this exact shade any other way.)

ACRYLIC PAINTS Like tempera, acrylics are water-based. They come in jars and tubes of bright colors (also at an art supply store). Jar paint is a lot like tempera; tube paint can be used much like oils. For long storage, this paint is also sold in pigments (powdered colors), to be mixed with water and an acrylic medium.

Use acrylics for painting and wherever you want <u>permanent</u> color. They dry very quickly, so

Clean your brushes immediately after using them. Check to see that they're wet while you've working, too!

Small jars of acrylics are handy to keep around for craft work. If you'd like to use them for art work, there are library books which will tell you more about this kind of painting. Here is one basic color list:

alizarin crimson (blue-red)
cadmium red light (orange-red)
cadmium yellow light (lemon yellow)
permanent green light (sunny grass green)
cerulean blue (warm blue on the turquoise side)
ultramarine blue (deep-ocean blue)
yellow ochre (brownish gold)
burnt sienna (warm reddish brown)
burnt umber (deep brown)
titanium or zinc white (a giant tube of it!)
black (optional)

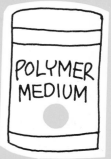

Acrylic paints dry to a dull finish. To make them shiny, go over them with polymer medium. This is a kind of "plastic varnish". It comes in a jar, looks like white glue when you're using it, and dries quickly and clear.

If you use acrylic paint in jars, rub some vaseline around the necks and lids when you first open them. This will keep them from sticking shut later!

WATERCOLORS

These are sold in cakes (usually in sets) and also in tubes. An inexpensive set from the dime store is good to keep on hand.

Usually watercolors are brushed on in washes— thin coatings of paint which you can see through. Use them over pencil drawings. Use them over marking pen drawings, too. (The edges will blur to give a special melted effect if you use water-base markers.)

For painting, watercolor paper is sold in art supply stores. It has a special bumpy texture to collect and "pool" colors in areas where you want them to go.

COLORED INKS

You'll find bottles of these at an art supply store. The colors are permanent and sometimes <u>very</u> bright. You can use them like water-colors and also for things like batiking. They work well for making designs on cloth, but will fade if the cloth is washed!

BLOCK PRINTING INKS

These inks come in tubes, with either water or oil bases. If you're a printer, you'll want to keep some around. They're sticky and work better than tempera or acrylic paints, especially on hard surfaces like linoleum blocks! Buy them in an art supply store.

FELT-TIPPED MARKING PENS

These have several different names: felt-tip pens, markers, magic markers and so on. They come in brilliant colors that dry quickly, in tips that range from ¼ inch to two inches. For general use, try the ¼ inch tip, depending upon how you use your small finger muscles. (You may want to try a larger size.)

You can buy markers almost everywhere. Inexpensive sets are sold in dime stores and wherever paper supplies are carried. If you want to try the permanent oil-base markers, you'll find up to 80 different colors in an art supply store. You can even buy an opaque white marker to soften the brightness of the other colors.

Markers pinch-hit for watercolors. Use water-base colors and go over them with a soft wet brush. They'll melt into paintings!

Try to keep water-base markers around for sketching. Take them when you go on trips. You can use them in bed (no water, no mess), on your lap, on the floor—even on long car rides. They're the best thing to come along since crayons! Keep them tightly capped so they don't dry out.

★ All paint is toxic (even tempera and watercolors) unless the label says specifically NON-TOXIC.

FOOD COLORING

Use food coloring like watercolors, to brush over paper as well as things like cream cheese. They come in small, somewhat expensive containers — to be used sparingly. Buy them in a grocery store.

JELLO

Mix small amounts of flavored gelatin with water until you have a slushy consistency. This can be brushed over paper for a shiny watercolor-like finish. Each flavor (and color) has its own smell, too. There's no blue yet, but you can substitute purple (grape)! Other colors are red (strawberry), yellow (lemon), orange (orange) and green (lime). You'll find variations on all of these colors, too!

This is a safe, pleasant-tasting paint substitute. (See "Food is beautiful", too.)

OIL PAINTS

Oil paints are the traditional artist's colors (although you can use acrylic tube colors a lot like them). They come in tubes and are sold at art supply stores. If you're a serious artist, be sure to try them. There are good books in the library on oil painting. A clerk in an art supply store can help you with the basic supplies, too.

Oil paints are permanent. You'll need turpentine to thin them (and clean up after them) and also linseed oil — it helps the thick color flow more easily. Canvas, canvas panels, heavy paper (like drawing paper or brown paper bags) cardboard and wood make good painting surfaces. If you use paper or cardboard, varnish it first so the paint won't sink in as deeply. A basic color list is under ACRYLIC PAINTS.

The greatest thing about oil paint is that it dries slowly — so slowly that you can build it up in layers, almost like thin clay — taking things out of a picture and adding them. It takes several days to dry thoroughly.

For a special way to paint with oils, see the next page.

The following come in NON-TOXIC forms: tempera, watercolors, water-base block printing inks and water-base marking pens.

This is a good starting palette knife

OIL PAINTING (continued)

Even people who have never painted before enjoy oil painting with a palette knife. It's a little like cake-icing and a little like finger-painting! (You can do this with acrylic paints in tubes, too.) This is a way to make beautiful paintings if you have any vision problems or if your fingers have trouble controlling a brush — or if you find it hard to make small lines and shapes. (There are lots of knives to choose from!)

Use stretched canvas or some other sturdy surface for palette knife painting.

ACRYLIC HOUSE PAINTS

ACRYLIC PAINT

People sometimes forget these paints for art work on large areas. Use them like acrylic paints you'd buy in an art supply store. They're thicker, but just as bright. (Some paint stores will mix almost any color you want, to order.)

Acrylic enamels are like oil-base enamels, but easier to control. (They wash up with water, too.) Colors are extra bright and come in semi-gloss and high-gloss, as well as mat (no gloss). Use the high-gloss over things like rocks and other projects where you want a shiny, washable surface — like card board boxes, wood constructions and of course, walls!

ACRYLIC ENAMEL

SPRAY ENAMELS

SPRAY PAINT

(See "Stencils" and "Cloth can be like paper".) These are usually oil-base paints. They come in a limited range of colors, but can be used for exciting stencil effects. They're also handy for things like wicker and wire and places where it's hard to work a brush. Use them outdoors only, downwind (so the spray doesn't blow back in your face) and with close attention to the arrow on the nozzle. (It's easy to spray a gust backwards!) Never hold a spray can at eye level, by the way.

For bright colorful paintings, keep your brushes clean!

SOME PAPERS TO USE FOR ARTWORK

WHITE DRAWING PAPER — in large, loose sheets, 18" x 24" or (better) 20" x 26". Buy separate sheets at an art supply store, or a ream (500 sheets) from a paper company. This is the best all-round paper for tempera painting. It will also take acrylics, watercolors, felt-tipped markers, pencil, pen-and-ink, pastels, crayons, and even spray paint!

Brown paper bags from the grocery store

WHITE BUTCHER PAPER
This comes in rolls, either from a butcher or from a company that carries school supplies

Brown wrapping paper from the dime store

Cut-up grocery store cartons

Cardboard, tag board, bristle board, poster board — all from an art supply store. These and others come in super-sizes and also assorted textures. Fun to look over on window shopping trips, too!

taped together news-papers

NEWSPRINT — a leftover roll from a local newspaper plant (call on printing days) lightweight absorbant doodling paper — especially for anyone who doodles faster than the paper supply can keep up with them!

PAINTING SUPPLIES

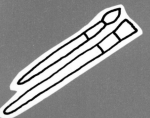

paper

rag

Painting is like cooking. It's more fun when you assemble what you need before you need it!

For most tempera or acrylic projects, these are things to have on hand:

1. Your choice of colors. Include the basic five: red, yellow, blue, black and white.
   - ✿ In tempera, add green, turquoise and magenta —if possible.
   - ✿ With acrylic paints, have both an orange-red ("cadmium red light") and a blue-red ("alizarin crimson").

2. Empty containers for small amounts of paint, also for mixing colors. For tempera, try paper cups in a muffin tin.

3. An empty coffee can for water.

* 4. Brushes, at least two – one which is flat and one which comes to a point when wet.
   - ✿ The younger you are, the larger your brushes can be.
   - ✿ If you have trouble using small finger muscles, use large brushes (also, see "Big brush painting").
   - ✿ If you have trouble holding a brush, tape it to your hand with paper surgical tape from a drugstore.

5. Paper for art work.

6. Paint rags or lots of paper towels for spills and clean-up; newspapers or a plastic cloth for work area—if needed.

7. Old painting clothes or a shirt-smock.

8. A cardboard box to store painting supplies when you're not using them.

* Tempera is recommended for all beginning painters and projects. When you use acrylic paint, rinse your brushes frequently and keep them wet. This kind of paint dries very quickly, and you can't wash it off!

(wear it backwards)

This is the recommended-size "round" brush for general use in painting. Buy it at an art supply store. Sable is the very best kind.

ABOUT SKETCH BOOKS

OIL PASTELS

Whether you've a realistic painter or you just like to make designs, keep at least one sketch book handy. Use it for spur-of-the-moment ideas. Try to work in it at least once or twice a week, too. You'll be surprised at the way your art work will develop with practice!

Work with marking pens, oil pastels (they're brighter than crayons and regular pastels), pen and ink or pencil — whatever you want. When you use color, have as many choices as possible.

You can buy a good drawing pencil at an art supply store. Drawing pencils are made with "B" soft lead — they'll have the letter "B" on them. (Spray drawings with a plastic spray to keep them from smudging.)

Carry your sketch book with you — indoors, outdoors, on trips! Some artists like to make sketches and use them for painting ideas. You may be one of them.

As you look through your sketch book you may find drawings you'd like to frame. When one sketchbook is filled, buy another to replace it!

THINGS TO DO WITH PAINTINGS

Tape them to a wall, door or refrigerator. (Be sure the tape you use won't pull off paint.) Glue them first to a sheet of colored paper, if you want.

Put one or two favorites in frames from the dime store. Rotate them with new paintings, if you want.

Tape a painting into a tube shape. Add yarn to make a decorative hanging.

Sew or tape several paintings into a scrapbook.

Wrap a present in a painting

Tape a painting over a dowell from a hardware store. Use yarn to hang it like a banner.

FUN FOR COSTUMES, CHRISTMAS TREES AND CELEBRATIONS!

Cut a painting into small shapes and folders. Save them for greeting cards.

You can also string the shapes and wear them. (Varnish over the tempera to keep it from rubbing off on clothes.)

Use a blunt-ended canvas needle to sew or string paper shapes.

More things to do with paintings

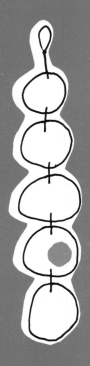

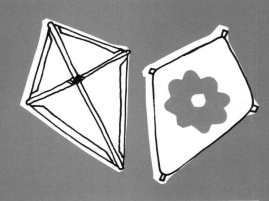

Make a painting into a kite!

Cut two or three paintings into strips. Glue or tape them together. Add words or other decorations. Tape the strip ends to paper towel tubes to make a scroll.

Make a "waterfall" of cut-out shapes from paintings.

to Rob

Make a painting into a letter. Write a message on the back. Fold it up and give it to a friend!

Tape two large sheets of cardboard into a "portfolio". Use it to keep paintings flat and safe.

A WORD ABOUT DRAWING BOARDS

You can paint wherever it's comfortable for you—at an easel, on a table, on the floor. You may enjoy using a drawing board, too.

A drawing board removes your work from some of the distractions around it, like cups of paint and other things you may be using. It holds your paper on an even working surface, and you can carry it to a sitting place. It's handy for painting on the floor (it raises the working surface) and for painting outdoors, too.

Art supply stores carry thick, lightweight boards. You can also have one made at a lumber yard (a 24" x 30" size is good) — or use a piece of masonite cut to size (tape the sharp edges). A metal clamp will hold your paper to the board.

POUR, SPILL, SPLASH

Sometimes the best way to enjoy paint is to put on old clothes and get as close to it as you can! Spread a large sheet of paper on the floor or any comfortable working surface. Cushion it on newspapers for spills, and set paints around you. Use different size brushes, if you have them — house painter's brushes if you have super-size paper! Here are some ways of working with paint. Try several ideas on the same sheet of paper, or experiment on different papers.

To make paint thin, add lots of water. To make it thick, add soap flakes. (This is one way to make finger paint, too!)

Try making paint "interesting". Add things like sand, sawdust, coffee grounds and shredded paper.

Make paint sparkle, too! While it's still wet sprinkle colored glitter over it. (Buy glitter at an art supply store, or at a craft and hobby store.)

If you'd like to experiment, but have trouble doing some of the things on these pages, you can have fun drizzling lines and shapes from a detergent bottle (the plastic squeeze kind). Fill the empty bottle with paint and water — about the consistency of light cream. (Use this kind of drizzling wherever painting is confined to a small area, too.)

SOAP FLAKES

COFFEE GROUNDS

Sponge it! To start, dip one end of a sponge in yellow paint and the other end in blue. Run a little green down the middle. Then press the sponge down for a melted rainbow look! Overlap sponge prints to make sun-on-water colors.

WHAT CAN YOU DO WITH PAINT?

Use other things besides brushes. Draw in paint with a stick!

Rake it with a comb!

"Butter" it with a knife!

Make lines in it with a fork!

Push it! Use a pancake turner or a piece of cardboard.

Blot it! Use paper towels or an old paint rag.

Mix it into colors on your paper! Use your fingers.

Spatter it! Use a paper drinking straw to blow big spatters into spidery lines.

(Paint should be thin to blow it)

To spatter: Run paint over an old toothbrush. Then scruff the toothbrush over the edge of a comb or paintbrush handle, directing the paint where you want it to go.

Hold your brush about two feet over your paper.

Drip paint!

Drizzle it!

Splash it!

Supplies:
- Tempera
- Brush
- Paper
- Lots of paper cups or empty containers
- Water

COLOR MIXING

This can be fun at any age - It's like working in a testing laboratory. Later, use all of the colors you've mixed in a painting!

RED and YELLOW make ORANGE.

BLUE and YELLOW make GREEN

Mix this the same way.

BLUE and RED make PURPLE

Start by putting a little red in a cup. Add some yellow and stir it around with a brush. If you don't like the first orange you see, add more color until it looks better to you!

Lots of blue will make grape purple. Lots of red will make a boysenberry purple. You may want to mix two!

RED, YELLOW and BLUE make BROWN

← Keep experimentin when you make brown - more of this, less of that - until you have just the color you want.

Do you know any grey cats? →

BLACK and WHITE make GREY

RED and WHITE make PINK

Sometimes this comes as a surprise!

RED and WHITE and YELLOW make PEACH (also, a WHITE SKIN color)

BROWN and WHITE make a MILK-CHOCOLATE color!

Two other popular colors to mix.

22

WHITE added to a bright color makes a "PASTEL" or an ICE CREAM COLOR

Special names for colors may help you to remember them better!

strawberry

raspberry

Peach

Lemon

lime

blueberry

Don't try to remember all of these color mixtures. It's important just to know that you can make them! If you paint a lot, some of them will come to you while you're working. You can always use this page for reference.

For artists who want to go further, here are some color recipes.

✿ To make a color lighter, add white.

✿ To make a color darker, you have two choices:

► Add black to any tempera color <u>except</u> yellow. (Black may turn it to a muddy green.) Add purple to yellow, instead.

► Or add the color's complement. Complementary colors are red and green (Christmas colors), yellow and purple (Easter colors), blue and orange (pumpkin and blue sky colors)! When you make a color darker this way, it'll be brighter than if you'd added black.

✿ To make an area or shape stand out, paint it darker than the colors around it.

✿ To push a shape into the background, paint it lighter than the colors around it.

Here's a word game. You can paint a rainbow from the letters in a man's name, ROY G. BIV! Each letter stands for a color, in rainbow order: R (red), O (orange), Y (yellow), G (green), B (blue), I (indigo) and V (violet). Indigo is a blue-purple. Violet is a red-purple.

$ FINGER PAINT

Supplies:
- Finger paint
- Finger painting paper from an art supply store, or shiny shelf paper (not the kind treated for bugs!)
- Scissors
- Glue
- Kleenex
- Brush
- Glitter
- Sponge

You can buy finger paint at an art supply store, or you can make your own. Mix one cup of liquid starch with one cup of powdered tempera (1/2 cup of liquid tempera). Or pour liquid starch over your paper and mix colors into it! Either way will work.

In a pinch, mix soap flakes with liquid tempera. For thick, sticky warm finger paint, make a pot of <u>wheat paste</u>* and add either powdered or liquid tempera to it!

Dampen your paper with a sponge. Spoon finger paint on the shiny side and spread it around with your hands and fingers. Play with the paint. Use your palms, knuckles, arms and elbows.

If for any reason you have trouble painting with your hands and arms, try using your feet and toes. (This is fun even without problems!)

Plants are fun to make in finger paint. So are fish. So are lines. Every time you squish into the paint, you'll make a design!

Mix colors on your paper while it's wet, or use Kleenex or a paper towel to lift a small spot of color. Then add a second color where you cleaned off the first. Do this with as many colors as you want.

MORE ABOUT FINGER PAINTING —

Try dipping your finger into different colors and using it like a brush. You can "write" in finger paint with a brush handle, too.

For extra sparkle, sprinkle glitter lightly over designs while the paint is still wet.

Finger paintings make good backgrounds for printing. Here's another idea: cut out designs in different colors from different papers. Glue them down on a single finger painting to make a collage! (See "Collages, all kinds!")

* To make wheat paste, mix one cup of flour and three cups of water. Stir the mixture over medium heat until it starts to boil. It'll turn transparent, too. Take it off the heat and let it cool until it can be handled. Then divide it into separate containers, and add a different color to each one. Use it while it's still warm.

Some people don't like the feeling of cold finger paint on their hands. Use this warm mixture, instead! For extra appeal, add a few drops of peppermint extract to make it smell good.

A FOOT PAINTING

Supplies:
- Tempera
- Brush
- Water
- Large sheet of paper (taped together if necessary)
- Crayon

Have someone trace the outline of your feet on a large sheet of paper – shoes on, shoes off, one foot at a time, both together, backwards, forwards, toes pointed in, toes pointed out – however you want! You can outline your socks, too!

If you use a crayon for the outlines, it will be easier to fill in shapes later with paint. (The wax in the crayon will hold back some of the paint like a fence.)

Fill in the outlines with bright tempera colors. Then fill in the spaces between the outlines. If you want, add stripes and dots and other designs to some of the foot and shoe shapes. You may want to glue on a few decorations, too!

A WALK-ALONG PAINTING

Supplies:
- Tempera
- Brushes (including large ones)
- Butcher paper, taped
- Water

A WALK-ALONG PAINTING – Unroll a sheet of butcher paper about six or eight feet long. Tape it to a second sheet for more width, if you want. (Use sheets of drawing paper if butcher paper isn't available.)

Start painting colors - bright ones - at one end of the paper. Don't worry about "designs" - you'll be making designs as you paint! Rinse your brush often to keep colors fresh.

Work your way across the paper - standing, sitting, crawling - whatever you feel like! Don't get tired, though. You'll be using lots of large muscles. Sit and rest every few minutes.

Your paper should be large enough to let you decide when to stop and when to go on. Fill it up with colors, or just cut off an end wherever you finish.

Supplies:
- Tempera
- Brush
- Paper
- Water

A BLOT PICTURE

Fold a sheet of paper in half. Open it up again. Paint thick colors on one side of the fold, stopping in the center. Press the other half of the paper over the paint to make a continuous design.

This is an easy way to make big beautiful multi-colored butterflies! ▶

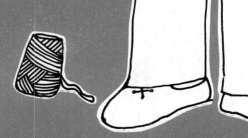

A STRING PICTURE

Fold a paper in half. Dip one end of a string in thick paint. Slip it inside the folded paper and let the other end hang out.

Press a second paper over the top to hold things in place. Then wiggle the string end. Snap it free and open your paper to see the designs you've made! Try using several strings with different colors! ▼

Supplies:
- Tempera
- String
- Paper

PRESS

PULL

PAINT

27

Big Brush Painting

Using house painters' brushes on large sheets of paper is fun for everyone. Many who have trouble holding and using smaller brushes can paint this way.

Tack butcher paper, brown wrapping paper, (or taped-together drawing paper sheets) to a piece of tag board. Prop the board against a wall for an easel.

Spread newspapers around the working area. Use pre-mixed or powdered tempera. (Keep powdered tempera-and-water mixtures fairly thick.)

Anyone who wants to keep going on super-size projects should try acrylic house paint for a permanent finish.

Think about painting groups of grocery store cartons different colors and assembling them. You can paint wood constructions and murals, too!

SEE YOURSELF, LIFE-SIZE

Unroll a sheet of butcher paper or whatever you've using. It should be at least three feet wide and two or three feet longer than you are.

Lie on your back. Have someone outline you. Get up and think about what you want to do with your outline. Make it realistic or just fill in the shape with colors. Or make yourself into someone else! It's fun to glue decorations to this kind of portrait, too.

Supplies:
• Butcher paper, brown wrapping paper or drawing paper (taped)
• Crayon or marking pen
• Tempera
• Brush
• Water
• Decorations
• Glue

29

NUMBERS, LETTERS, SHAPES

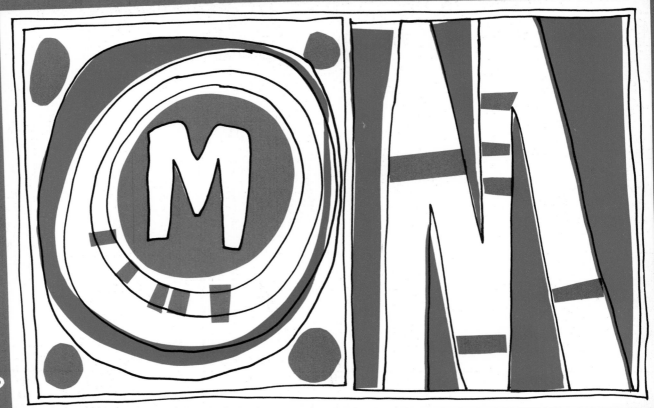

Supplies:
- Tempera
- Brush
- Water
- Paper
- Numbers letters and shapes for reference
- Felt-tipped markers, chalks, crayons

Beautiful paintings and drawings can be made with simple shapes.

You can start with your own name - or just letters. Change the colors and sizes of the letters, work them around corners, repeat them in rows - big rows, little rows - march letters off the paper bring them back on the other side, make them FAT make them SKINNY, curve *them*, stretch them OUT, shorten them, loop some letters into others, paint boxes around them ! Use chalks, crayons, markers and paint if you want. Or just use paint. You can do the same things with numbers and simple shapes (circles, triangles, squares).

Most people can paint circles. Try making them in different colors all over your paper. Fill in the spaces between the colors. Or try just one circle, one number or one letter and see how you can work color around it!

There are endless design possibilities with this kind of doodling. You may be surprised at all the things you can make!

BATHTUB PAINTING

Supplies:
- Tempera (for easier clean-up mix it with a little liquid detergent)
- Brush
- Bathtub or sink
- Sponge and cleanser for clean-up

★ You should be large enough to paint comfortably over a tub, ("kneeling in front of it") not in it! Lots of people have trouble doing this kind of thing, too. If you're one of them, paint a sink, instead!

Bathtub painting is fun because it's different, also because it relates object painting to flat art work. (It's a good rainy day activity, too!)

Paint your way around a tub or sink in bright colors. Paint a figure in the tub—or a fish, or some animal. Paint leaves. Or flowers. Or just colors. Work loosely and don't spend much time on this—especially if your arm starts to get tired!

Have someone take a picture of you and your work. This is a way of recording art that isn't permanent. Any good cleanser will wash the paint away quickly. Enjoy the different colors as they blend together with water and run down the drain.

IN AND UP, UP AND DOWN, OVER AND UNDER

Supplies:
- Tempera
- Brush
- Paper
- Water
- Felt-tipped markers, chalks, crayons (optional)

Like waves, like wind, like little snakes inching their way over paper, brush strokes can repeat themselves into designs. Sometimes these are called rhythms. Fill up a painting with one.

You can express all kinds of motions with rhythms. Fast. Slow. Excited. Calm. You can paint rain and waterfalls and even slow-moving snail rhythms. Use different colors as you paint and try moving your whole arm, not just your fingers. Add chalks, crayons or marker designs over the paint, if you want. (Let the paint dry first, though!)

EASY FACES

Supplies:
- Paper
- Felt-tipped markers

 SE✋+

Draw a circle.

Add two dots for eyes.

Add a line for a mouth.

Happy face.

Unhappy face.

Draw circles around the eye dots.

Eyes left

Eyes right

Eyes up

Eyes down

where are your eyes going?

It's fun to add eyelashes and eyebrows.

Mad eyebrows

Sad eyebrows

Make more realistic eyes in leaf shapes.

LEFT NOSE   RIGHT NOSE

Noses are hard to draw. (The Egyptians tried not to draw them at all!) Experiment with nose shapes. Here are a few to try.

Here's one basic mouth shape. (Think about two hills and a lake, or a bowl of ice cream.)

For another kind of face — Glue magazine cut-outs into a circle. Add paper scraps for hair.

33

STICK FIGURES

Supplies
- Paper (lots of small sheets)
- Felt-tipped marker

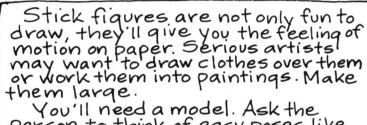

Stick figures are not only fun to draw, they'll give you the feeling of motion on paper. Serious artists may want to draw clothes over them or work them into paintings. Make them large.

You'll need a model. Ask the person to think of easy poses like hitting a baseball. Draw their action in a stick figure. (It's hard to stay in a pose very long, so put a pile of paper in front of you and plan to work as quickly as you can.)

Even if you think you can't draw at all, you may be surprised at how well you can draw stick figures!

If you want to add details to a stick figure, go ahead. Give the circle a face, or draw clothes over it. Or just leave it like it is!

The next time you want to paint a figure, think of what the body is doing under the clothes. If you want, draw a stick figure first and then paint over it.

It's fun to glue several stick figure drawings on a large sheet of colored paper. You'll have something that looks like an action cartoon!

P.S. If you have any vision problems, try drawing on dark paper with a fat piece of white chalk.

CONTOUR DRAWING

Supplies:
• Paper
• Felt-tipped marker

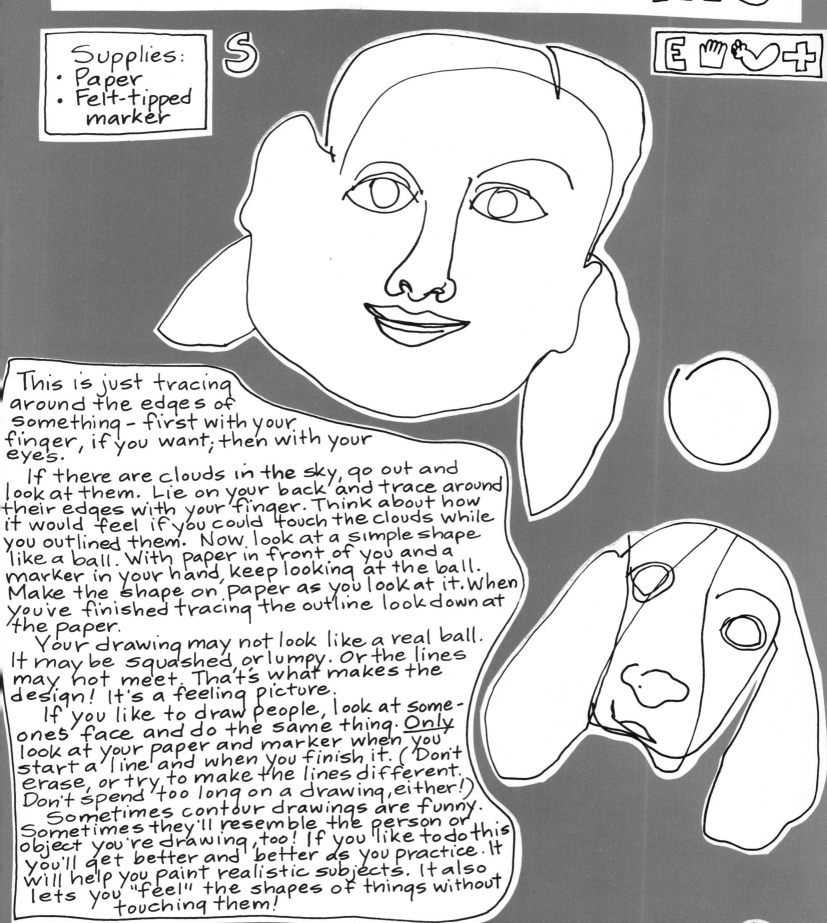

This is just tracing around the edges of something - first with your finger, if you want; then with your eyes.

If there are clouds in the sky, go out and look at them. Lie on your back and trace around their edges with your finger. Think about how it would feel if you could touch the clouds while you outlined them. Now look at a simple shape like a ball. With paper in front of you and a marker in your hand, keep looking at the ball. Make the shape on paper as you look at it. When you've finished tracing the outline look down at the paper.

Your drawing may not look like a real ball. It may be squashed or lumpy. Or the lines may not meet. That's what makes the design! It's a feeling picture.

If you like to draw people, look at some-ones face and do the same thing. Only look at your paper and marker when you start a line and when you finish it. (Don't erase, or try to make the lines different. Don't spend too long on a drawing, either!)

Sometimes contour drawings are funny. Sometimes they'll resemble the person or object you're drawing, too! If you like to do this you'll get better and better as you practice. It will help you paint realistic subjects. It also lets you "feel" the shapes of things without touching them!

WHAT CAN I PAINT?

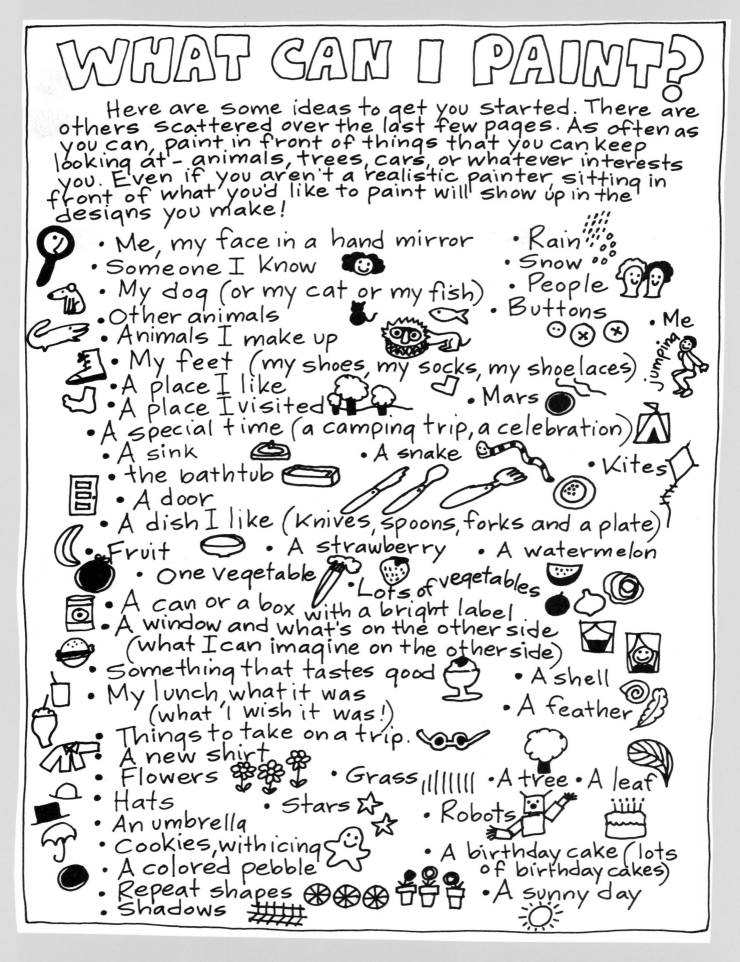

Here are some ideas to get you started. There are others scattered over the last few pages. As often as you can, paint in front of things that you can keep looking at - animals, trees, cars, or whatever interests you. Even if you aren't a realistic painter, sitting in front of what you'd like to paint will show up in the designs you make!

- Me, my face in a hand mirror
- Someone I know
- My dog (or my cat or my fish)
- Other animals
- Animals I make up
- My feet (my shoes, my socks, my shoelaces)
- A place I like
- A place I visited
- A special time (a camping trip, a celebration)
- A sink
- the bathtub
- A door
- A dish I like (knives, spoons, forks and a plate)
- Fruit
- One vegetable
- A strawberry
- A watermelon
- Lots of vegetables
- A can or a box with a bright label
- A window and what's on the other side (what I can imagine on the other side)
- Something that tastes good
- My lunch, what it was (what I wish it was!)
- Things to take on a trip.
- A new shirt
- Flowers
- Grass
- A tree
- A leaf
- Hats
- Stars
- Robots
- An umbrella
- Cookies, with icing
- A colored pebble
- A birthday cake (lots of birthday cakes)
- Repeat shapes
- A sunny day
- Shadows
- Rain
- Snow
- People
- Buttons
- Me jumping
- A snake
- Mars
- Kites
- A shell
- A feather

POTATO STAMPING

Supplies:
- Potatoes (raw)
- Knife
- Tempera
- Brush
- Paper
- Water

Cut designs into a raw potato, as shown. For easy handling, cut them into a chunk of potato. You can carve them into smaller shapes, too.

There are two ways to print with potato stamps. Run a brush and paint over a design and then print it. Or soak a few paper towels in paint and use it as a stamping pad. (This is easier if you have trouble holding a brush.)

Stamp small shapes together to make border designs. Use lots of colors and over-lap some shapes. Make designs over old paintings and finger paintings. Make wrapping paper and greeting cards. Cut a potato in a blade-of-grass shape. Stamp lots of blades into a lawn. Stamp flowers over it. Stamp butterflies, moons, stars, suns! These are only a few of the things you can do with potato stamps! (Also, see "Inner tube cut-outs.")

★ Potatoes are easy to cut. So are hands! Let someone else do the cutting, if necessary!

37

INNER TUBE CUT-OUTS

Supplies:
- Old inner tubing
- Scissors
- Glue
- Cardboard or wood scraps
- Paint
- Brush
- Paper
- Mat knife, block-printing ink, optional (see below)

   Inner tube cut-outs are like potato stamps, but you can keep them indefinitely. You can also glue shapes over other shapes to make a "relief" print. Paint or ink your design and place a sheet of paper over it. Rub gently over the paper with the back of a spoon, then pull up your print!
   Look for an old inner tube in a garage or gas station. Car salvage lots almost always have them.
   You can cut inner tubing into shapes with a pair of sharp scissors. Glue them down on heavy cardboard or small wood scraps.
   If you're able to use a mat knife (from an art supply store), you can cut more intricate shapes—even an alphabet! Stamp the letters into words on Japanese rice paper. (You can glue your letters on small wooden cubes. A lumber yard will cut them for you.) Cut all letters in reverse.

MAT KNIFE

A BRAYER

★ Mat knives require good coordination and special handling!

For professional looking prints, use water-base block printing ink and a brayer. Make an inking plate from a piece of glass with taped edges or a sheet of aluminum.

QUICK MONOPRINTS

This is fast, easy, bright art!
Use glass from an old picture frame, or buy an inexpensive piece from a glass company. Tape the edges securely.

There are different ways to make monoprints. Here are three of them. You'll probably think of others as you experiment!

Supplies:
• Tempera
• Pane of glass with taped edges
• Paper
• Scissors

Spread paint over the glass.

Lay cut or torn paper shapes and string over the paint. (Paint them different colors first, if you want.) Press paper over them. Lift it up for a print.

You can use block printing ink for monoprints, too!

Cut a large, simple stencil. Spread paint over the glass and lay the stencil on top of it.

Make designs in the paint that will show through the paper stencil, then press a paper over everything. Lift it up for your print.

Spread a thin layer of paint over the glass. Use your finger or a stick to make lines and shapes in it.

Press a paper over the paint. Pull it up to make a print!

39

LINOLEUM BLOCK PRINTS

L E 🖐+👁 ★

Supplies:
- Linoleum blocks or sheet linoleum
- Linoleum block cutter
- Block printing ink
- Brayer (roller)
- Glass pane or aluminum foil

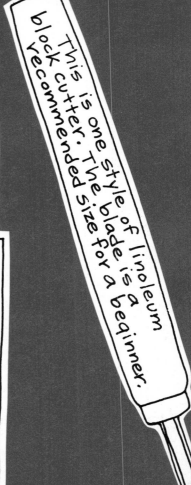

This is one style of linoleum block cutter. The blade is a recommended size for a beginner.

★ A project for those with good coordination and patience! Close supervision is needed for all cutting. (Make sure the linoleum is heated before cutting.)

You can make beautiful prints with linoleum blocks. For many, it's a first step into the pleasures of graphics – woodcuts, lithographs, silk-screen prints (serigraphs) and etchings.

Buy a linoleum block in an art supply store or a craft and hobby shop. When you're ready to work on it, heat it in a 200 degree oven for about 10 or 15 minutes – or until the surface cuts easily. When it starts to get hard again, put it back in the oven.

Work intuitively, or draw a design first and then trace it on the linoleum block.

40

You can make just lines, or you can scoop out some areas and leave others alone. Whatever you scoop out will print WHITE. Whatever you leave alone will print DARK.

There are different size cutters (or gouges) – big ones for wide lines and small ones for narrow lines. A recommended size is shown.

It's important to cut with one hand over the other hand, or in front of it. Point the blade away from you, too! This may seem awkward at first, but it's safer!

When you've finished your lines, shapes or design, squeeze block printing ink over a taped piece of glass or aluminum foil. (A cookie sheet works, too.) Run a brayer (roller) back and forth a few times until it's coated with ink. Then run it over the linoleum.

Press paper over the block and rub over it with the back of a spoon. (You can pull up edges while you're rubbing, to make sure you haven't missed a spot.) Use pressure! Paper with a little texture, like white drawing paper, will print better than one that's very smooth – but experiment!

It's fun to print the same design in different colors. You can make two-color prints by cutting two different blocks and printing them on the same paper. You can also cut a simple design, like a heart shape, and print it in different colors on the same paper!

↳ This is the print.

↳ This is the linoleum.

DARK areas are cut out.

Cut with one hand over the other, or in front of it! Always point the blade away from you!

41

STRING PRINT

Supplies:
- String (thick)
- Paper
- White glue
- Scissors
- Paint
- Brush for Paint

Dip string in glue or run a glue outline over your paper and press the string into it. Either way, make a design in string.

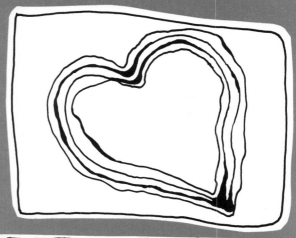

Let the glue dry. Then run thick paint over the string. Don't worry if some of it slips over on the paper.

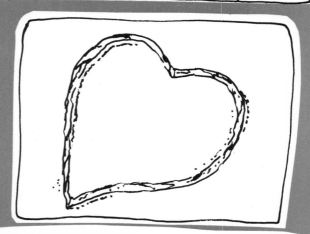

Press a clean sheet of paper over the wet paint. Run your fingers over the string outline, then pull up the paper for a print.
For fun, finish painting the paper that has string on it. Add more string and decorations if you want. Now you have both a print and a collage!

SWIRL PRINTS

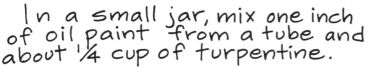

Supplies:
- Shelf paper
- Shallow pan
- Water
- Oil paints in tubes
- Turpentine
- Eye dropper
- Clothespins
- Rubber gloves (if needed)

In a small jar, mix one inch of oil paint from a tube and about ¼ cup of turpentine.

Fill an eye dropper with the paint mixture and pour drops over water in a shallow pan. Use as many different colors as you want.

Clip a clothespin to a piece of shelf paper (for easy handling). Then lay the paper gently on the water and let it float for a moment.

For super-swirl prints, clip clothespins to both sides of your paper and hold them while you move it end to end.

Lift out your print and let it dry flat.

Swirl prints are beautiful by themselves. You can use them for gift wrapping papers, book jackets, collages, printing papers and even to cover cardboard loop bracelets!

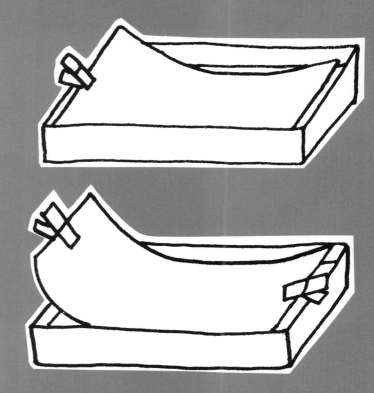

★ Oil paint is hard to remove from clothes. Turpentine looks like water, blinds if splashed in eyes and kills if swallowed. Don't take your eyes off it.

If there's any question about these materials, mix powdered tempera and vegetable oil. Spoon this over water for another kind of swirl print.

CRAYON PRINTS

Supplies:
- Paraffin
- Paper
- Paint
- Brush
- Water
- Iron

PARAFIN

IRON

★ An iron should be used with close supervision!

This is fun, especially if you have some flowers to look at while you're working. You don't need them, though. You don't even have to draw flowers - you can just make designs.
  Fold a large sheet of paper in half. Draw on one side of fold with a thick chunk of paraffin (from a grocery store). Re-fold the paper and iron over it with a warm - not hot - iron. This will transfer your wax designs to the other side of the fold. You'll have a continuous pattern.
  Paint over one or both sides with watery tempera. Your wax shapes - or flowers - will show through! P. S. You can do this on a piece of white cotton, too.

HOME MADE "CLAYS"

Different people sometimes enjoy different kinds of clay. The easiest kind to make is Baker's clay. It has a lot of salt in it, which may make someone who swallows it sick. But it won't hurt you.

Mix together:

Four cups of flour, one cup of salt and one and ½ cups of water.

Knead the mixture like dough until it's pliable, adding more flour or water, if needed. Make it into fairly flat shapes on aluminum foil — flatten the foil first on a cookie sheet. Bake at 350° for one hour or until hard and toasty-looking.

Baker's clay will puff up a little in the oven, just like bread. Parts of shapes may shrink, too. Be ready for surprises!

For small beads and other objects, Cornstarch clay won't puff up or shrink. You can let it air-dry:

Mix one cup of salt, ½ cup of cornstarch and ¾ cup of water in the top of a double boiler. Put in the salt and cornstarch first, then add the water SLOWLY. Heat it until it's thick, then let it cool on a piece of waxed paper. When it can be handled, knead it for a few minutes. Then it's ready to go!

Salt + cornstarch + water

Flower and leaf shapes — Make dots and lines with a toothpick. ▼

Flat Baker's clay Pin made from Baker's clay. Clasp ▶ is baked into the back!

Flat "Pendant" — make "hair" by pushing Baker's clay through a garlic press! Hanging loop is a hairpin. ▶

▲ Pencil puppet with cornstarch clay head and yarn hair. Wrap-around cloth scrap is anchored with string.

Dog and hippopotamus — Make details with a toothpick. Paint Baker's clay and cornstarch clay with acrylic ◀ paint. Varnish or shellac ▶ over it to make colors shine! Your

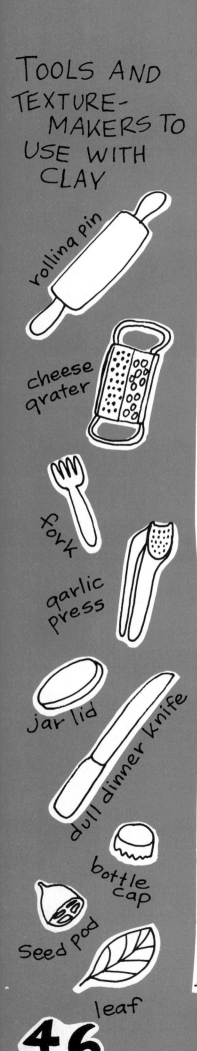

TOOLS AND TEXTURE-MAKERS TO USE WITH CLAY

rolling pin

cheese grater

fork

garlic press

jar lid

dull dinner knife

bottle cap

seed pod

leaf

USING COMMERCIAL "CLAYS"

It's good to know that there are other kinds of modelling materials for sale in art stores and craft and hobby shops. Some are self-hardening; others have to be baked. A new product (one brand name is "Sculpy") is a little like Baker's Clay, but it bakes without puffing up or shrinking. "Sculpy" is non-toxic, but there are other mixtures that aren't. (All commercial clay should be checked for toxicity.)

NATURAL CLAY

Natural clay is clay from the ground. It has lots of different names: Indian clay, potter's clay, moist clay. It's sold in white and earth colors. Most people like to work with the earth color. Buy it in an art supply store, or directly from a potter. Store it in a container with a tight-fitting lid, or in a plastic bag that can be tied off tightly. Keep it in a cool place, adding water drops to it from time to time (to keep it moist).

Natural clay dries hard, but it will slump back into its original form if it gets wet. Protect it with acrylic paint, varnish, shellac, liquid floor wax, polymer medium (the acrylic varnish—use it over acrylic paint or by itself) and even colorless nail polish. If a kiln is handy and you plan to fire it, make sure the air bubbles are out of the clay before you shape it. Use a string or wire to cut a chunk of clay. Throw it down on a flat surface. Knead it. Pound it. Do this until you can cut through the clay and it's smooth (no small air pockets showing)! This is healthy, big-muscle activity, by the way!

Natural clay rubs off—on people, on clothes, on tables. It rarely stains, but it's a good idea to wash it off as soon as possible.

There are three traditional ways of working with clay: ball, slab and coil. All of them are on the next few pages.

CLAY PICTURES

L

Supplies:
- Clay
- Rolling pin
- Old dinner knife
- Pencil or drawing tool
- Leather thong (optional)

Roll out clay with a rolling pin or a thick dowel. Cut shapes in it like the ones shown.

Draw a design on the clay. Stamp a few textures on it, if you want. To make a hanging plaque, poke holes for a leather thong.

Let the clay harden. Paint it with acrylic paints and use polymer medium or varnish to seal the open places. (Seal the clay even if you don't paint it.)

If you can fire the clay in a kiln, low-firing glazes come in fairly bright colors. Use these to paint your design.

String plaques, as shown. Clay pictures can be mounted on wood scraps, too.

Roll out clay.

Cut out a clay shape.

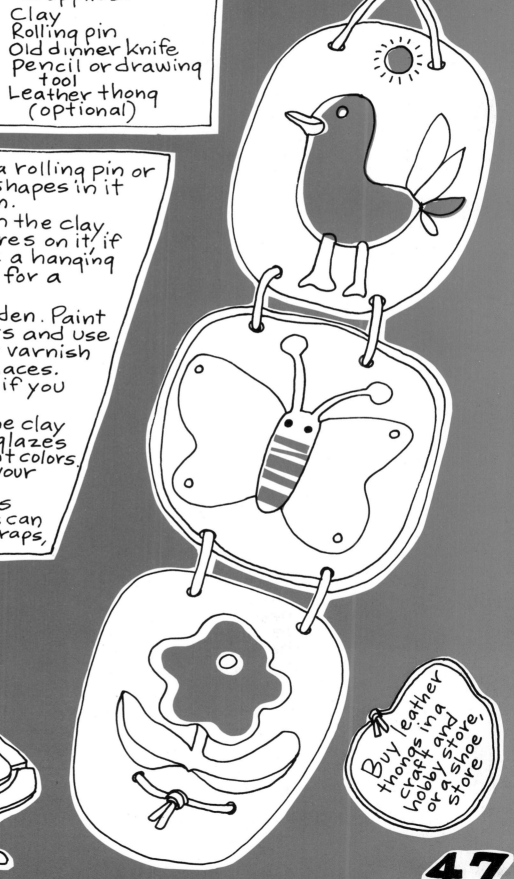

Buy leather thongs in a craft and hobby store, or a shoe store.

THUMB POTS

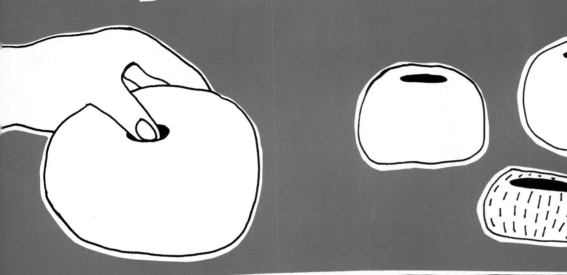

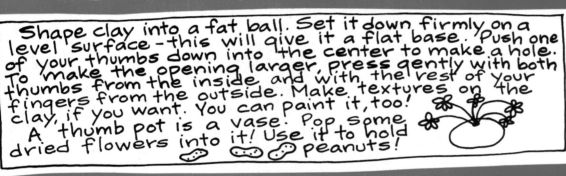

Shape clay into a fat ball. Set it down firmly on a level surface - this will give it a flat base. Push one of your thumbs down into the center to make a hole. To make the opening larger, press gently with both thumbs from the inside and with the rest of your fingers from the outside. Make textures on the clay, if you want. You can paint it, too!

A thumb pot is a vase. Pop some dried flowers into it! Use it to hold peanuts!

SNAKES

Roll a lump of clay between your palms. Stretch it out and shape it into a coil. Pull up the inside end for a head. Make eyes with a tooth-pick.

Make lots of snakes! Paint them different colors and varnish over them to make them shine.

A coil snail

a sleeping snake

CLAY BEADS AND BIRDS

Make large fat balls of clay (about the size of those above). Stick a toothpick through the center of each one. Wiggle it around to make the opening larger - and leave it in the bead if you want to paint it later.

Make birds the same way. Work each ball into a lumpy shape and use a toothpick to make eyes and other details. Let it dry.

Paint and varnish clay before you wear it. Or string beads and birds with other things (like driftwood) for decorative hangings.

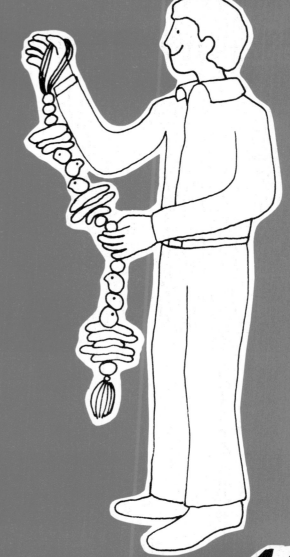

49

EASY CLAY FIGURES

E 🤚 V

Roll a ball of clay for a head. Roll a larger ball for a body. Stretch it out a little. Roll clay between your palms to make fat "snakes"! Break off pieces for arm and leg shapes.

Make details with a toothpick.

Stick the shapes together.

Pull the arms in toward the body, or anchor them so they won't fall off later!

Roll out a long flat body shape. Roll out a flat hair shape and form a ball for a head. Form the flat body shape into a cone. Attach the head to the smallest open end. Fold the hair over the head. You can make this kind of figure with or without arms.

COIL BASKETS AND EGGS

beak

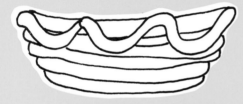

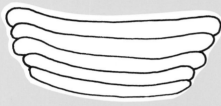

Make coil vases this way, too.

Make a coil (see "Snakes"). Smooth it over, if you want. Build up the sides with more lengths of clay, until your clay shape starts to sag a little. Smooth it over or leave it like it is. Set it aside to dry while you make eggs and a chicken.

Make a fat ball of clay to fit your basket. Work it into a lumpy shape and make eyes with a toothpick. Use a pencil tip to make "feathers". Let it dry.

Paint and varnish over your shapes. Then put the eggs in the basket and the chicken over the eggs!

CLAY AND SCRAP MATERIALS

S

It's fun to experiment with clay and different scrap materials.

Here, clay plus toothpicks, plus a face poked into it turned out to be Murray's porcupine! It stands up, too!

A lump of clay.

Toothpicks

51

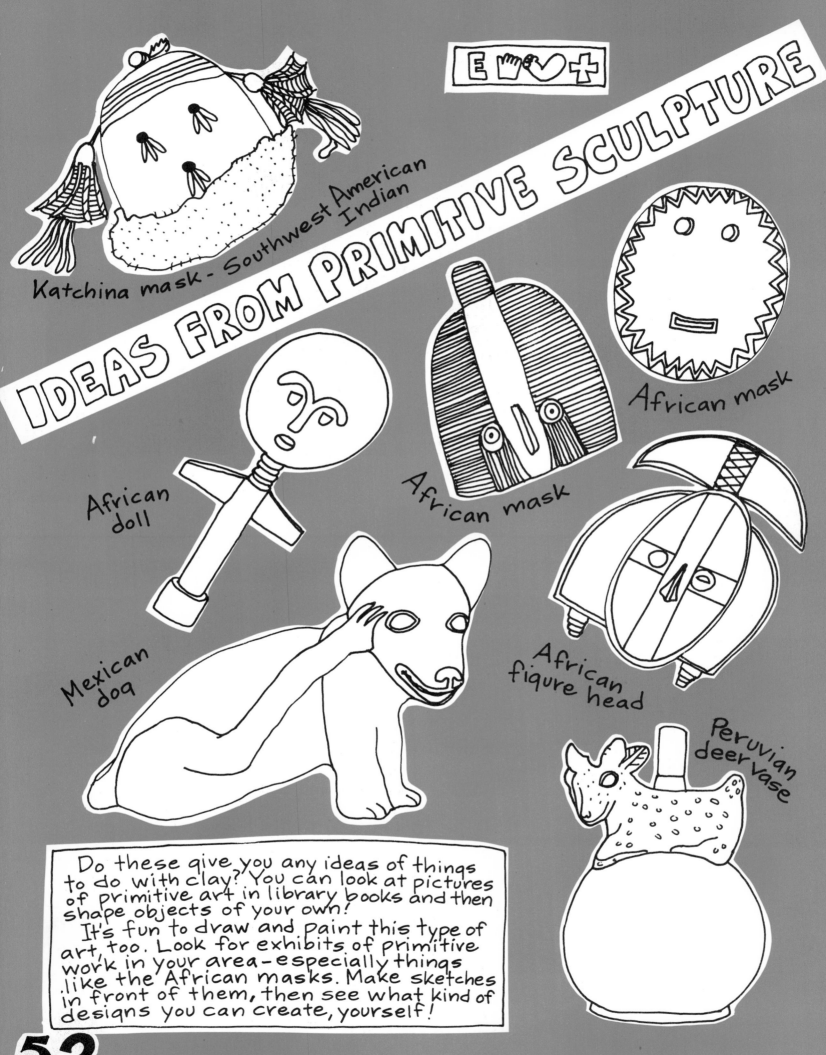

IDEAS FROM PRIMITIVE SCULPTURE

Katchina mask - Southwest American Indian

African doll

African mask

African mask

Mexican dog

African figure head

Peruvian deer vase

Do these give you any ideas of things to do with clay? You can look at pictures of primitive art in library books and then shape objects of your own!

It's fun to draw and paint this type of art, too. Look for exhibits of primitive work in your area—especially things like the African masks. Make sketches in front of them, then see what kind of designs you can create, yourself!

FOOD IS BEAUTIFUL, TOO
WHIPPED CLOUD PIE

Supplies:
- Baked pie shell
- Pie filling
- Whipped cream
- Paper cups
- Food coloring
- Chocolate sprinkles or other decorations

Put this masterpiece together for a special occasion. It's expensive (if you use real whipped cream), but it's beautiful!
    Fill a baked pie shell with something good - canned cherry pie filling, pumpkin filling, fresh strawberries. The larger the pie shell the better. If you have a pizza pan, use it to make a double recipe of pie crust!
    Whip at least two pints of cream and divide it into bowls. Add a different food color to each bowl (mixture instructions are on the food color box). Stick to lighter shades unless you don't mind eating bright green and blue, etc.! If you have a cookie press, spoon the cream into it. Otherwise, poke a hole in the bottom of a paper cup and spoon some cream into that. Then pinch the bottom of a second cup to make it fit the first. Press it down, so the cream comes out of the hole like toothpaste! (Make several cup sets, so you can use one with each color.) Build designs with the whipped cream up to a daisy center. Top it with a cherry, chocolate sprinkles or even a daisy (wash it off, first). Take a picture of your art work to record it, then have a good time eating your pie!

53

BREAD BEAST

E 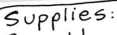 + L

Draw a pattern to fit your cookie sheet, or work intuitively!

Supplies:
- Bread dough
- Cookie sheet(s)
- aluminum foil
- Large sheet of paper
- Pencil or marker
- Caraway or poppy seeds

Follow a basic recipe for white or egg bread, with yeast. (You can use pretzel dough, too.) Knead it well, let it rise, then knead it again. Divide the dough into sections. It helps to have a pattern or some idea of how you want to shape it - but you can work intuitively, too! Keep things very simple because the dough will rise, and you'll lose small details.

Let the dough rise again until it doubles. Then brush over it with a mixture of one egg plus about a tablespoon of water. This will make the top crusty brown and shiny.

The beast shown is about half size. The eyelashes are caraway seeds. For distinct lines, like the legs, leave about a 2 inch space between dough shapes. Wherever things like eyes were added, the dough underneath was punched down to make a place for them.

Enjoy your bread beast while it's warm - with butter and jam!

DECORATED PIZZA

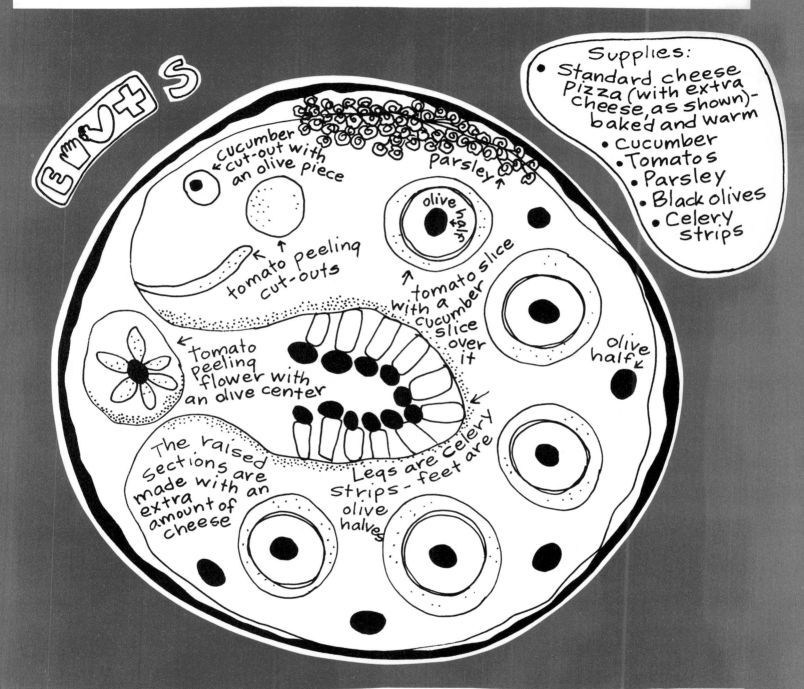

ENVT S

Cucumber cut-out with an olive piece

Parsley

Supplies:
- Standard cheese Pizza (with extra cheese, as shown)- baked and warm
  - Cucumber
  - Tomatos
  - Parsley
  - Black olives
  - Celery strips

olive half

tomato peeling cut-outs

tomato slice with a cucumber slice over it

Tomato peeling flower with an olive center

olive half

The raised Sections are made with an extra amount of cheese

Legs are Celery strips- feet are olive halves

Here's a caterpillar pizza. It doesn't sound good, but it is! More than that, you can eat your art work, pizza and a salad — all at the same time.

Before the pizza is baked, build a raised shape out of extra cheese. This can become a caterpillar outline. Work quickly on the hot pizza, pressing vegetables into it for decorations. (Take a picture of your art work to record it.) Then eat it!

This may give you ideas of other ways to decorate food. If you don't want to make realistic shapes, work in repeat patterns and designs.

PAPIER-MACHE

A free form shape

Supplies:
- Wheat paste (see recipe under "Finger paint")
- Newspapers
- Tape and/or string
- Paint
- Brush
- Varnish and brush

You can tear up newspapers into strips and dip them into wheat paste to cover almost anything!

One idea is to roll newspapers into tubes, as shown, and tape and tie them into animals and figures – or just interesting shapes. (You don't have to make newspaper forms look like anything except newspaper forms! Paint will transform them into bright designs.)

Cover a newspaper framework with torn newspaper strips about 1" x 4" or 5". (Tearing instead of cutting helps the paper to stick more easily.) Dip them first in wheat paste. Run at least two layers of strips over a surface – three are better. Then put your work aside to dry two or three days.

Paint over your shape with just tempera, if you want. For a more professional finish, run polymer medium or gesso (a thick white paint from an art supply store) over it. Paint it with acrylic paint.

Either way, varnish over paint to make it shine! Add decorating scraps, too, if you want

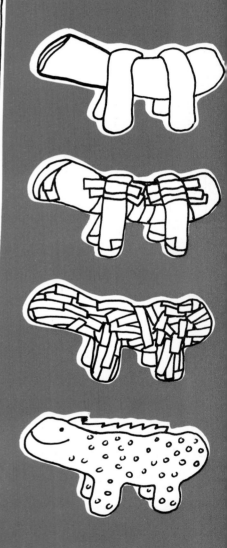

Above: the basic newpaper form; a taped form (you can use string, too); the form covered with newspaper strips; and the finished form, painted, varnished and decorated with a cloth scrap!

FLAT PAPIER-MACHE

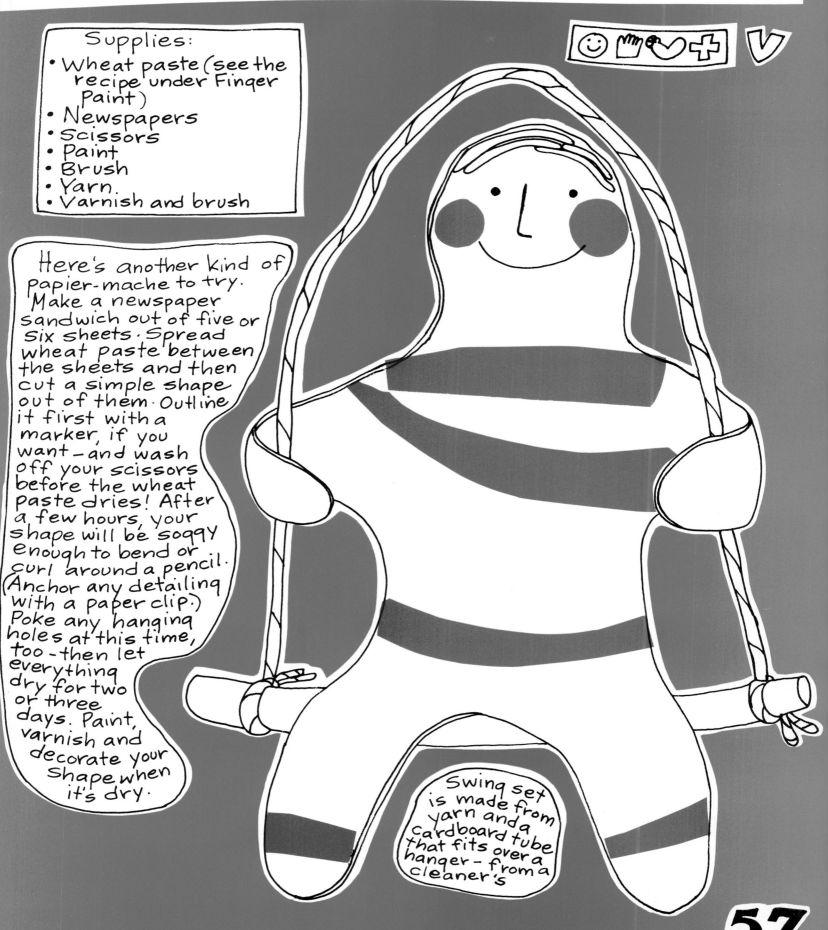

Supplies:
- Wheat paste (see the recipe under Finger Paint)
- Newspapers
- Scissors
- Paint
- Brush
- Yarn
- Varnish and brush

Here's another kind of papier-mache to try. Make a newspaper sandwich out of five or six sheets. Spread wheat paste between the sheets and then cut a simple shape out of them. Outline it first with a marker, if you want — and wash off your scissors before the wheat paste dries! After a few hours, your shape will be soggy enough to bend or curl around a pencil. (Anchor any detailing with a paper clip.) Poke any hanging holes at this time, too — then let everything dry for two or three days. Paint, varnish and decorate your shape when it's dry.

Swing set is made from yarn and a cardboard tube that fits over a hanger — from a cleaner's

57

PAPER SHAPES AND CUT-OUTS

Supplies:
- Paper (large sheet)
- Scissors
- Paint
- Brush
- Marking pens
- Glue
- String
- Glitter, other decorations

GLUE

butterfly

caterpillar

   Look at pictures of bugs. Most of them can be drawn in simple shapes and lines!
   Choose a shape you like. Draw it first, if you want. Think about how you want it to look.
   Cut a bug shape out of a large sheet of paper. Glue on any extra parts, like legs or wings.
   Color your bug with paint or marking pens, or both. Add any extra decorations, like colored paper and glitter (see the opposite page).
   Hang your bug on a long piece of string. A clothespin will fasten it to things like the top of a curtain. A piece of masking tape will hold the string on a ceiling.

firefly

Pincher bug

pretend. potato bug

Spider

dragonfly

bee

centipede

beetle

lady bug

ant

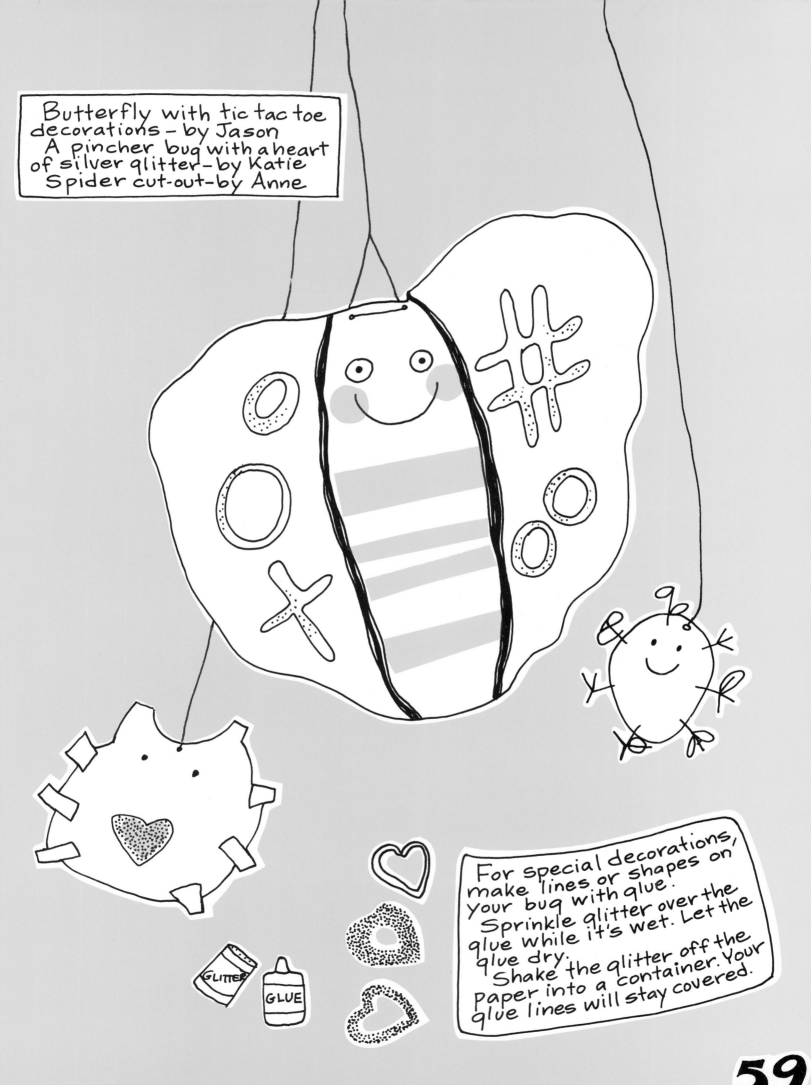

COLLAGES

Basic supplies:
- Paper, all kinds
- Glue
- Scrap objects that will glue flat (like buttons)

The word collage comes from a French word meaning "to stick." A collage is a picture made up of different things stuck together. Different kinds of collages are scattered through this book. Here are some ideas for collages that are mostly paper.

Cut some simple shapes out of white paper. Paint them in bright colors! Then glue them on a second paper, adding more designs around them, if you want!

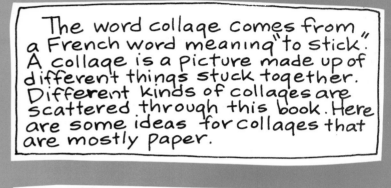

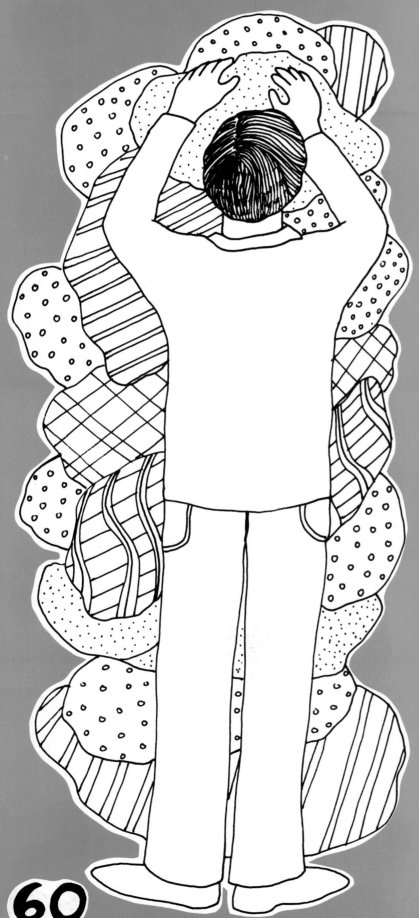

◄ If you have a super-size paper, think about collaging it with shapes cut (or torn) from a wall paper sample book! (They're usually free for the asking.) Run bright paint into your collage, if you want.

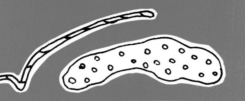

These are the things collages are made of - paper scraps, cloth scraps, leaves, string, magazine illustrations, tin foil, gum wrappers, packaging material! Find them inside and out-side.

Lay one thing down on a sheet of paper. Decide where you want it, then glue it in place and do the same thing with the next piece. Make realistic shapes or just work in designs.

For a special collage, fill your paper with shapes - but don't glue them down. Instead, press clear, sticky Contact paper over everything!

Cut a large paper in the shape of a suitcase. On a separate paper, draw or paint things to take on a trip - like brush, toothbrush, socks, doughnuts. Cut them out and glue them on the suitcase shape. Add paint and scrap decorations.

Cut or tear pieces of newspaper. Make a ▶ design with them or just glue down shapes. Try glueing them on black paper and add paint, if you want.

Cut big simple shapes out of colored paper. Glue them on a sheet of white paper. Lay a sheet of colored tissue paper over them, then brush polymer medium (or glue mixed with water) over the tissue paper. Add more shapes and more tissue paper, if you want. Go over them with more polymer medium or glue. (Tissue paper will blur a little when it's wet, by the way.) ▶

CEREAL COLLAGE

SUGAR BIRD

This is a texture picture. You can feel its design as well as see it!

Work intuitively, or use a marker to make shapes on a sheet of paper or cardboard.

Spread glue over one of the shapes you've drawn. Then sprinkle one kind of cereal over the glue — let it dry for a few minutes before shaking off the excess cereal. Go on to the next section, spreading glue over it and dropping another kind of cereal — or seeds, or beans, or whatever you have. Keep going until you've filled in all of your shapes!

Sugar Bird was the only outline on the collage shown — the other shapes were filled in around it. (You might want to try a Powdered Jello Bird, Salt Bird, Coffee Bird or Crushed Peanut Bird!) The bird's eye is a Cheerio.

Preserve a cereal collage with a coat of polymer medium or varnish.

Supplies:
- Different kinds of cereals, seeds beans, sugar and other textures
- Heavy paper or cardboard (large sheet)
- Glue
- Marker

WOOD CONSTRUCTION

Supplies:
• Wood scraps
• Glue
• Nuts, bolts, hardware
• Paint, brush
• Paper
• Scissors
• String and other decorating scraps
• Varnish

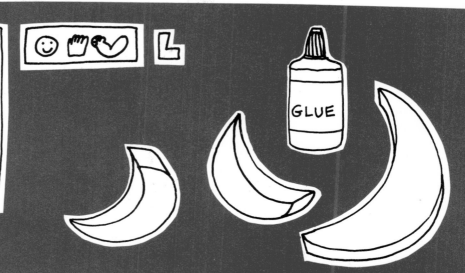

Look through a lumber yard scrap bin, or ask a cabinet maker for some of his "turned" pieces (like those above). Hold some of the wood scraps in your hand. Do they remind you of anything? Think about some of the primitive art you may have seen, like African masks made of wood.

You may enjoy just glueing scraps together intuitively. Use white glue, and let your work dry overnight, if possible. Add hardware and other decorations, if you want. Then go over everything with polymer medium or varnish-to make it shine!

Wood constructions can be simple and small, or super-size pieces of sculpture!

WEAVING

E ✋💚✝ L

Tie five thick strands of yarn to a low tree branch or wherever you can reach it easily. (If you don't have thick yarn, use three or four strands of regular yarn, per color.)

Take the first strand of yarn on the right and pass it alternately over and under the others. Now do the same thing with the yarn strand that's left on the right, and keep on going.

Tie off the bottom end. Tie off the top, and then cut the top loops. Tie a few jingle bells or other decorations at the bottom.

This makes a bright door hanging!

P.S. You can use seven, nine or eleven strands if you find you like weaving and want to try a thicker piece.

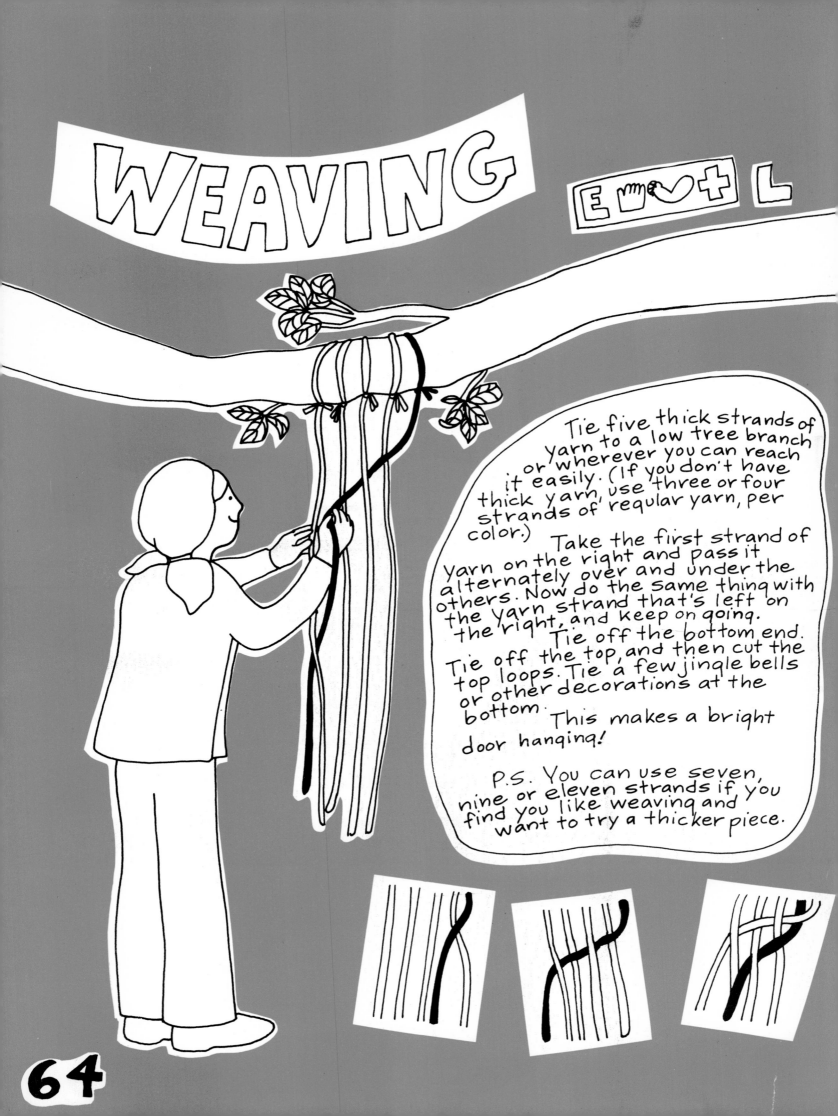

BROOM PUPPET

Supplies:
- Broom
- Brown paper bag
- Newspapers
- Glue
- String
- Scissors
- Paint or markers
- Brush
- Tape

Wrap newspapers over a broom and tape them in place. Tie a paper bag over the newspaper stuffing. Cut out strips of newspaper and glue them to the bag for hair. Make a face with paint or markers, and add any other decorations you want. Give your character a name! This kind of puppet is large enough to pop over bushes or into doorways!

The same kind of puppet made over a pencil. Use a cloth scrap tied over cotton!

STICKS AND STONES

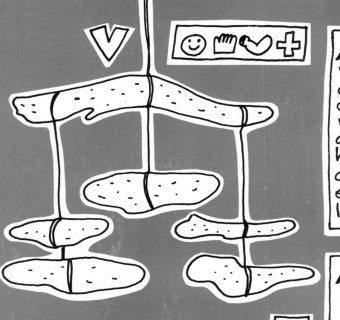

▶ Some "sticks" are beautiful, especially weathered ones like those you find along a beach or in an old forest. You can make hanging decorations and mobiles from driftwood. (See "Beads and birds" in the section on clay.) Use a hand drill to make holes in flat pieces, or tie them in place. Mobiles are effective strung on transparent fishing line (hardware stores carry it).

▶ Look at a stick. Does it remind you of anything? Will painting or decorating it make it look more like a special figure or object? You can glue sticks together into designs, too. Mount them on scrap wood or use them for hanging pieces.

◀ You can make fetish dolls out of sticks, too. Decide where you want a face (if you want a face) and mark two dots for eyes. Then decorate the rest of a stick with paint and scraps—yarn, string, paper, cloth and ribbon. Tie on small objects like bells, beads and seed pods.

◀ Stone figures are fun to make. A little stone on top of a big one usually looks like a head on some kind of body. All you have to do is decide what kind of body you want it to be! Add paint, then varnish—if you want your figure to shine.
▽ The stones below are painted as lady bugs and strawberries, and in dots and patterns. (You might want to add a face or two!) These decorative rocks can be displayed in groups. Be sure to varnish over them—the shine is part of their appeal!

TIN CANS AND BOTTLES

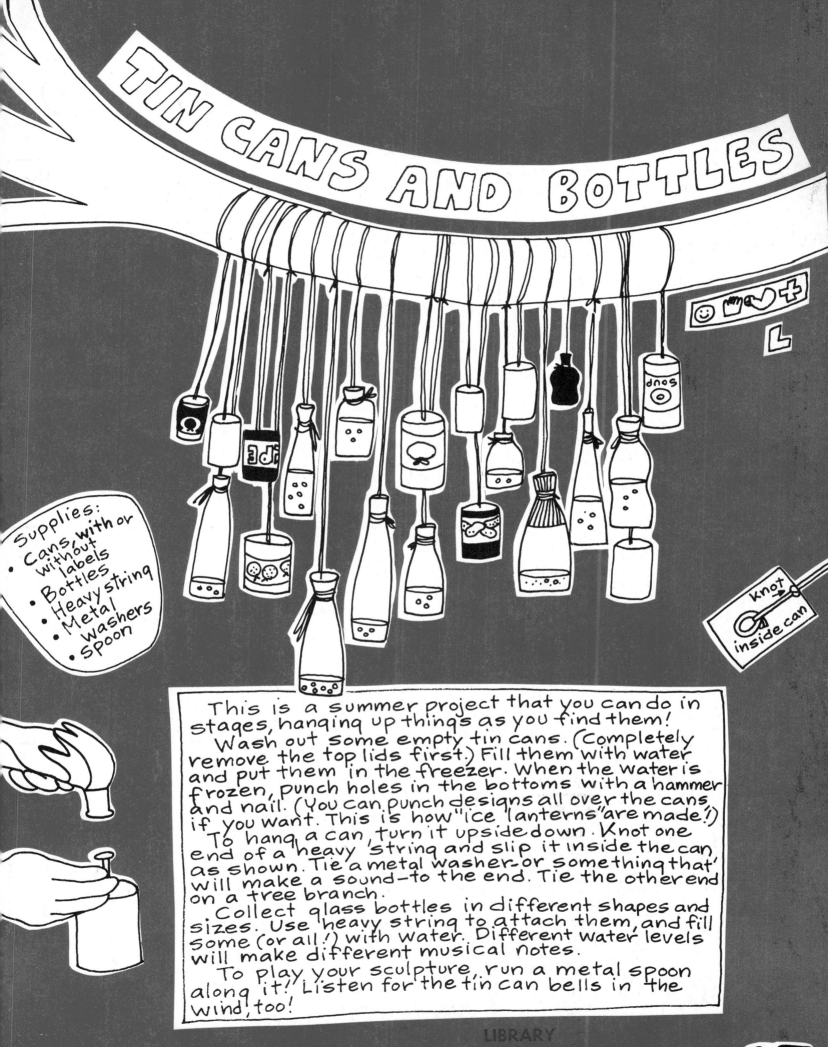

Supplies:
- Cans, with or without labels
- Bottles
- Heavy string
- Metal washers
- Spoon

knot inside can

This is a summer project that you can do in stages, hanging up things as you find them!

Wash out some empty tin cans. (Completely remove the top lids first.) Fill them with water and put them in the freezer. When the water is frozen, punch holes in the bottoms with a hammer and nail. (You can punch designs all over the cans if you want. This is how "ice lanterns" are made!)

To hang a can, turn it upside down. Knot one end of a heavy string and slip it inside the can, as shown. Tie a metal washer—or something that will make a sound—to the end. Tie the other end on a tree branch.

Collect glass bottles in different shapes and sizes. Use heavy string to attach them, and fill some (or all!) with water. Different water levels will make different musical notes.

To play your sculpture, run a metal spoon along it! Listen for the tin can bells in the wind, too!

SAND SCULPTURE

Supplies:
- Sandy beach
- Found objects - sticks, stones, seaweed, shells, beach glass

Find a place on the beach where the sand is dry on the top, but still a little damp underneath. This is the easiest sand to move into shapes. (Don't work too close to the water unless the tide is going out!)

If you don't want to work with damp sand, just stretch out anywhere. Lie in the sun for a few moments and think about ways you can shape the area around you.

Use your arms to build up gentle mounds. Decorate them with things you find on the beach. You may want to make something realistic, like a fish or a mermaid—or a long winding snake shape. Paper cups filled with damp sand make interesting dragon-teeth and buildings.

Have someone take a picture of you next to your art work to record it!

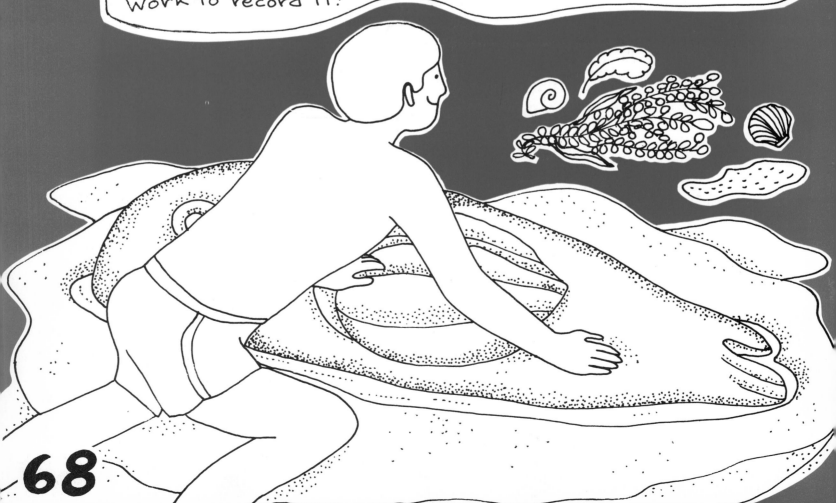

SAND CASTING

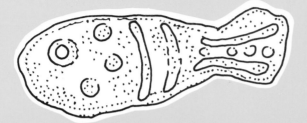

Supplies:
- Beach, or box of sand, about 6" deep
- Plaster of Paris
- Bowl or bucket
- Water
- Spoon
- Rubber gloves

This is fun to do at a beach! Find an area of damp sand near the water, which isn't in danger of being washed over. Try to work at low tide, or where you'll have at least an hour to let plaster set.

If you aren't near a beach, fill a cardboard box with sand. Dampen it with enough water to hold a shape.

Use your hands to make a shape in the sand. Scoop it out carefully. Whatever you do on the inside will show later on the outside. Press small objects like shells and marbles into the mold, if you want.

Fill a bowl or bucket with water (sea water if you're at the beach). Put on rubber gloves and start adding plaster to the water. Sprinkle it over the water like flour, crushing any lumps. When the plaster stops sinking and starts floating on top, you've mixed enough!

Work quickly and gently, pouring plaster into your sand shape. If you want to hang your shape later, imbed a hanging string or wire loop into it.

Let your shape dry at least an hour at the beach, and overnight in a box. (If you're at a beach, cushion it on something soft for the trip home. It will be fragile until it's dried thoroughly.) Then brush off the sand and see what appears!

P.S. It's interesting to feel plaster while it's first drying. It will be cool and then warm and then cool again!

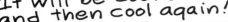

BANNERS

Supplies:
- Burlap (hem the edges or pull them) – or felt
- Cloth scraps
- Glue *
- Scissors
- Wooden dowel
- Yarn
- Decorating scraps

* Although spray glues are tempting for cloth, they're dangerous and <u>not</u> recommended. Use white household glue, instead.

GLUE

    Cut a piece of burlap or felt to the size you want. Then cut cloth scraps into shapes and designs that will fit it. Glue them into place. Glue on string or paper or any other decorations you may want.
    Stitch or tape the top of the burlap over a dowel. (Felt can be glued.) Tie yarn at each end of the dowel, then hang your banner on a wall!
    P.S. The selection of colors, the placing and the glueing are the most important things in banner-making. Let someone else put the structure together, if necessary.

CLOUDS

Supplies:
- Soft shiny satin, in white or pastels
- Stuffing material
- Sewing supplies
- Scissors
- Paper, pencil
- Plastic fishing line

This is soft sculpture — cloth shapes meant to be enjoyed as art work. Make them like any stuffed shapes. (See "Cats and other easy dolls".) Draw a paper pattern for each cloud and cut two identical pieces of cloth to match the pattern. Stuff them lightly and suspend them from the ceiling on transparent fishing line (look for it in a hardware store). Attach the line to a thread loop on the seam line of each shape.

Satin is soft and glistens a little — you'll enjoy looking at it! Can you think of other soft sculpture to make?

CLOTH CAN BE LIKE PAPER

E ✋ ♥ ✚

L You can paint anything you want on cloth, especially tightly-woven cotton.

Keep your paint about the consistency of thick cream. Before you start, slip cardboard under your working surface. Pin the cloth firmly to the cardboard to hold it in place. Work on an even place, like a table. Use acrylic paints. Wash painted cloth in cold water with a little salt.

An acrylic paint design

An acrylic "wash" design - turn your cloth upside down and let thin paint run over it. Add more colors, let them run over the first! Keep turning the cloth until you have all the color you want.

A design with oil-base markers. Draw an outline first and fill in color on both sides of the cloth.

Use stencil paper from an art supply store.

Cut out this part

An acrylic stencil design

Spray-Painted clouds

SPRAY PAINTING ★
Spread cloth on newspapers. Pin paper over any area you want to stay unpainted. Slip cardboard into any clothing to keep the paint from seeping through. Pin paper cut-outs to the cloth. Test spray paint first on newspapers, then spray gently over your cut-outs. (You may want to work with someone else at spraying, both of you holding the can.) Let the paint dry a little, then move the cut-outs and try a second color. Try spray painting with leaves, too! ★ See "Paints".

STRINGING THINGS TOGETHER

People have been stringing things for centuries - for jewelry, for costumes, for decorations. Here are a few ideas that you can try.

Paper shapes strung with a needle and thread. For a thicker necklace, make them out of flat papier-mache.

Life savers on licorice - you can eat this one!

Macaroni in different shapes and sizes - dunk it in food coloring, if you want. It can be spray painted, too. ★

A flower necklace - or "lei". Bend a piece of thin wire, like this  to make a needle. Use sewing thread, but wax it first by running it over the end of a candle or parafin.

- Leaves
- sardine key
- driftwood
- key chain
- orange peels
- popcorn
- sliced paper tube
- magazine illustrations glued on cardboard
- vegetable slices
- wood shaving
- cornstarch beads
- leather thongs
- buttons
- jingle bells
- shell
- newspapers

Try some of these for costumes!

★ See "Spray paints."

BATIKING

Batiking is the art of making designs on cloth, usually with hot wax and cold water dyes. Some ways of batiking are simple! Others require a lot of skill. If you enjoy this as a starter, there are library books on batiking which go into great detail. Work with someone else and do all the steps, or just the ones you feel you can do best. The excitement comes when the wax is removed from the cloth!

Supplies:
- Paraffin
- Coffee can
- Electric frying pan
- Empty picture frame, or waxed paper, pins
- Cloth (cotton)
- Pencil
- Brush
- Ladle
- Hot pad holders
- Batik dyes, or double-strength RIT
- Bowl or bucket for mixing dye
- Long-handled spoon, or stick for stirring dye
- Rubber gloves
- Plastic or glass container for dye, or a sink (no metal)
- Clothesline, clothespins

The hot wax method makes the brightest batiks. If you have good finger coordination, you may want to try it.

Melt two chunks of grocery store paraffin in a coffee can set into an electric frying pan. Use hot pads to handle the can. If the wax starts to smoke, turn off the heat and let it cool down.

The wax is ready when it drips quickly off the end of a brush. It also will run clear lines over the rim of the can. (If the lines are milky, let it heat a while longer.)

You can brush or ladle hot wax on your cloth. If you use a brush, you may want to draw a design first. (Use a soft pencil.) Stretch the cloth over an empty picture frame, or put waxed paper under it and cushion it on newspapers. With ladling, it's fun to use a fairly large piece of cloth and work outdoors over waxed paper.

Be very careful applying hot wax. It can burn easily!

★ Use batik materials with caution, whatever the level of skill. Hot wax is flammable and can cause severe skin burns. Batik dyes are toxic, in addition to being permanent. Dye fumes should not be breathed!

CLOTH

→ WAXED PAPER UNDER THE CLOTH

WAX

WAX

WAX

NEWSPAPER CUSHION →

A one-color batik banner— hang it against light for a stained glass effect. ▶

Let the wax dry.(Crumple it a little if you want thin, spidery lines of color to form later over the areas it's covering.) Wherever you wax will stay white.

Put on rubber gloves and mix the dye according to the directions on the package. Be careful not to inhale the powder. Dip the waxed cloth in the dye. When the color is two or three shades darker than you want it rinse it thoroughly and hang it up to dry. (The color will get lighter as it dries.)

To remove the wax, iron it out between a thick sandwich of paper towels or newsprint.

To add more color, brush or ladle hot wax over the first color after the cloth has dried. (Don't iron out the old wax.) Dip the cloth in a second color, let it dry again - then iron out the wax.

INK

You can make batik without hot wax! Mix flour and water together until it can be squeezed out of a plastic detergent bottle to make thick lines. Draw a design with the mixture, and let it dry. Then paint over it with colored inks. When the inks have dried you can add more designs then more inks. When you've finished, scrape off your flour lines and set the color with a warm iron.

CATS

AND OTHER EASY DOLLS
E ✋ ♥ + L

Supplies:
- Cloth
- Stuffing material
- Sewing supplies
- Scissors
- Felt scraps
- Felt-tip markers
- Glue
- Decorating scraps

Cut two identical shapes out of cloth (kettle cloth comes in bright colors and is easy to work with.)

Sew the shapes together with a small running stitch. Leave an opening. Fill the inside with shredded foam rubber, cloth scraps or some other stuffing.

Sew up the opening.

For cats, cut two ears and a tail from felt. Sew them to the body. Dog's ears look like this — hands can look like this!

Use felt-tipped marking pens for a face — or glue on cloth details.

Stuffing and decorating this kind of doll are more important than the shape.

Use an old pillowcase or a simple cloth rectangle if cutting a free shape is difficult.

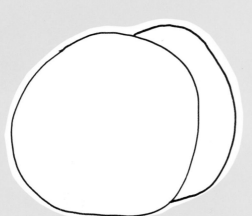

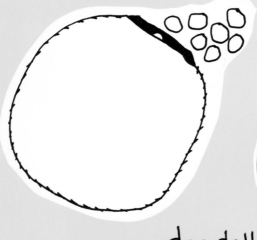

dog doll

Margo's doll— sewn-on hands and ribbon, marking pen face and hair.

Fat cat

Smiley Cat

Raq Cat

77

LET'S HEAR IT FOR 😊E✋♥✚ CELEBRATIONS!

Who needs a celebration? Everybody!

We celebrate holidays that are on the calendar, but what about one that isn't on a calendar?

What about Fresh Tomato Day? Penguin Day? Yellow Day? Sit-In-the Grass Day? What about Kite Day, Beach Day, Paper Bag Day, Sandwich Day, Crazy Hat Day, Apple Pie Day? Birthdays can be celebrated for anyone, anything, anytime. Everybody enjoys a personal celebration, too. It doesn't *have* to be a birthday.

What can you do on a made-up holiday? Put your art skills to work! Sometimes the holiday, itself, will tell you what to do. If it's Beach Day, have a party at the beach and try some sand casting or sand sculpture. Or bring the beach indoors by taping sheets of brown wrapping paper on the walls and painting it! Spread a blanket on the floor and have a picnic without going anywhere!

On Crazy Hat day, made paper hats or decorate old ones. Take pictures to record your work. Bake apple pies on Apple Pie Day—different kinds. Paint pictures of apples and wear them. You can paint apple cheeks on your face. This is the way many legitimate holidays started—people just wanted a party!

Keep celebrations fairly short and bright. No matter how simple the effort, everyone can contribute. A rule of thumb is to satisfy as many of the senses as you can—seeing, hearing, tasting, smelling, feeling. Paint and paper can set the mood for almost any holiday you can create. Use them generously!

APPLE PIE DAY

PAINT